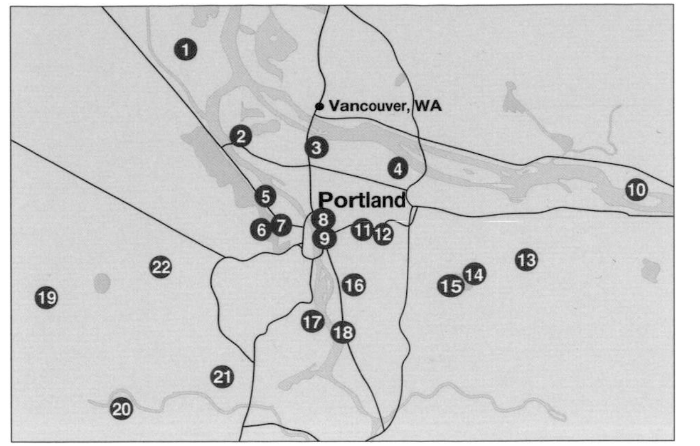

1. Sauvie Island
2. Cathedral Park
3. Peninsula Park & Rose Garden
4. The Grotto
5. Forest Park
6. Hoyt Arboretum
7. International Rose Test Garden
8. Lon Su Chinese Garden
9. Tom McCall Waterfront Park
10. Columbia River Gorge National Scenic Area
11. Laurelhurst Park
12. Mount Tabor Park
13. Gresham Japanese Garden
14. Powell Buttes Nature Park
15. Leach Botanical Garden
16. Crystal Springs Rhododendron Garden
17. Tryon Creek State Natural Area
18. Elk Rock Garden
19. Copper Mountain Nature Park
20. Tualatin River National Wildlife Refuge
21. Cook Park
22. Tualatin Hills Nature Park

Hoyt Arboretum

International Rose Test Garden

The Grotto

Measurements denote the height of plants unless otherwise indicated. Illustrations are not to scale.

N.B. – Many edible wild plants have poisonous mimics. Never eat a wild plant or fruit unless you are absolutely sure it is safe to do so. The publisher makes no representation or warranties with respect to the accuracy, completeness, correctness or usefulness of this information and specifically disclaims any implied warranties of fitness for a particular purpose. The advice, strategies and/or techniques contained herein may not be suitable for all individuals. The publisher shall not be responsible for any physical harm (up to and including death), loss of profit or other commercial damage. The publisher assumes no liability brought or instituted by individuals or organizations arising out of or relating in any way to the application and/or use of the information, advice and strategies contained herein.

Made in the USA

Waterford Press produces reference guides that introduce novices to nature, science, outdoor recreation and survival. Product information is featured on the website:
www.waterfordpress.com

Text and illustrations © 2020 by Waterford Press Inc. All rights reserved.
Images © Shutterstock.

To order, call 800-434-2555.
For permissions, or to share comments, e-mail editor@waterfordpress.com.
For information on custom-published products, call 800-434-2555 or e-mail info@waterfordpress.com.

ISBN 978-1-62005-440-6
$7.95 U.S.
UPC
10 9 8 7 6 5 4 3 2 1
205701

PORTLAND TREES & WILDFLOWERS

Kavanagh/Leung

A POCKET NATURALIST® GUIDE

PORTLAND TREES & WILDFLOWERS

A Folding Pocket Guide to Familiar Plants

Lodgepole Pine
Pinus contorta To 80 ft. (24 m)
Needles are twisted in bundles of 2. Cone scales have a single prickle near their outer edge.

Ponderosa Pine
Pinus ponderosa To 130 ft. (40 m)
Long needles are in bundles of 2 or 3. Cones have scales that have sharp outcurved prickles.

Sitka Spruce
Picea sitchensis To 160 ft. (49 m)
Flattened, sharp-tipped needles grow singly along hairless branchlets. Ragged cone has scales with wavy edges.

Western White Pine
Pinus monticola To 100 ft. (30 m)
Needles are in bundles of 5. Cones are up to 9 in. (23 cm) long.

Western Redcedar
Thuja plicata To 175 ft. (53 m)
Drooping branchlets are covered with overlapping, scale-like leaves. Small cones have woody scales. Bark is fibrous and shredded.

Douglas-Fir
Pseudotsuga menziesii
To 200 ft. (61 m)
Flat needles grow in a spiral around branchlets. Cones have 3-pointed bracts protruding between the scales. **Oregon's state tree.**

Grand Fir
Abies grandis To 200 ft. (61 m)
Flexible needles grow in 2 rows. Upright cylindrical cones have scales which are more broad than long.

Western Hemlock
Tsuga heterophylla To 230 ft. (70 m)
Tree top droops at the tip. Flat needles grow from 2 sides of twigs, parallel to the ground.

Common Juniper
Juniperus communis To 4 ft. (1.2 m)
Needle-like leaves grow in whorls of 3 around twigs. Berry-like, blue-black cones have 1–3 seeds.

Yellow Cedar
Chamaecyparis nootkatensis
To 100 ft. (30 m)
Scale-like leaves grow along 4-sided twigs that grow in flattened, fan-shaped sprays. Grayish cones are round.

Horse Chestnut
Aesculus hippocastanum
To 70 ft. (21 m)
Small flowers are succeeded by spiny green balls. Seeds are poisonous. Introduced ornamental.

Tree of Heaven
Ailanthus altissima To 80 ft. (24 m)
Introduced species is a widely planted ornamental. Dense clusters of yellowish flowers are succeeded by papery keys. Introduced from China.

Western Yew
Taxus brevifolia To 50 ft. (15 m)
Scarlet berries have protruding, greenish seeds. Leaves and seeds are toxic.

Cascara Buckthorn
Rhamnus purshiana To 30 ft. (9 m)
Shrub or small tree has leaves widest beyond the middle. Tiny white flowers are succeeded by black berries.

Trembling Aspen
Populus tremuloides To 70 ft. (21 m)
Long-stemmed leaves rustle in the slightest breeze. The most widely distributed tree in North America.

Bigleaf Maple
Acer macrophyllum To 70 ft. (21 m)
Drooping flower clusters are succeeded by winged seed pairs.

Vine Maple
Acer circinatum To 25 ft. (7.6 m)
Toothed leaves usually have 7–11 lobes. Fruit is a winged seed pair. Leaves turn red or yellow in fall.

Pacific Willow
Salix lasiandra To 50 ft. (15 m)
Narrow leaves are green above, grayish below.

Black Cottonwood
Populus trichocarpa To 120 ft. (36.5 m)
Flower clusters are succeeded by oval capsules containing cottony seeds.

Oregon White Oak
Quercus garryana To 70 ft. (21 m)
Distinctive leaves have 5–9 deep lobes. Acorn has a shallow, scaly cup.

Pacific Madrone
Arbutus menziesii To 80 ft. (24 m)
Red-brown bark continuously peels away, exposing smooth inner bark.

Oregon Crabapple
Malus fusca To 30 ft. (9 m)
Fragrant white flowers bloom in late spring and are succeeded by small, oblong apples.

Yaupon
Ilex vomitoria To 20 ft. (6 m)
Alternate, evergreen leaves have wavy-toothed edges. Flowers are succeeded by red, berry-like fruits that persist into winter.

Western Dogwood
Cornus nuttallii To 50 ft. (15 m)
Tree puts on a spectacular spring floral display. White petal-like leaves surround a small disk of greenish flowers.

Red Alder
Alnus rubra To 100 ft. (30 m)
Shrub or tree often forms dense thickets. Flowers bloom in long clusters and are succeeded by distinctive, cone-like woody fruits.

Oregon Ash
Fraxinus latifolia To 80 ft. (24 m)
Leaves have 5–7 large leaflets. Flowers are succeeded by distinctive winged "keys." Gray bark is deeply furrowed.

Bitter Cherry
Prunus emarginata To 20 ft. (6 m)
Shrub or tree. Clusters of white spring flowers are succeeded by bright red berries in summer.

Southern Magnolia
Magnolia grandiflora To 80 ft. (24 m)
Large creamy flowers, to 8 in. (20 cm) in diameter, have 9–14 petals. Cone-like, hairy fruits have bright red seeds.

Sweetgum
Liquidambar styraciflua
To 100 ft. (30 m)
Small, greenish flowers bloom in tight, round clusters and are succeeded by hard fruits covered with woody spines.

Hazelnut
Corylus spp.
To 10 ft. (3 m)
Sheathed, nut-like fruits mature into edible filberts by autumn. **Oregon's state nut.**

Douglas Spraea
Spiraea douglasii
To 5 ft. (1.5 m)
Narrow leaves are toothed on their upper half. Showy pink flowers bloom in a dense cylindrical cluster.

Oregon-grape
Mahonia aquifolium
To 10 ft. (3 m)
Leaves have spiny edges. Yellowish flowers bloom in loose clusters and are succeeded by edible blue berries. **Oregon's state flower.**

Mock Orange
Philadelphus lewisii
To 10 ft. (3 m)
Flowers have a heavy scent similar to orange blossoms.

Common Chokecherry
Prunus virginiana To 20 ft. (6 m)
Cylindrical clusters of spring flowers are succeeded by dark, red-purple berries.

Salmonberry
Rubus spectabilis
To 7 ft. (2.1 m)
Showy pink to purple flowers bloom June–July and are succeeded by red, raspberry-like fruits.

Thimbleberry
Rubus parviflorus
To 6 ft. (1.8 m)
Maple-like leaves are 5-lobed. Flowers are succeeded by lumpy red berries.

Himalayan Blackberry
Rubus armeniacus
To 10 ft. (3 m)

Red-osier Dogwood
Cornus sericea To 10 ft. (3 m)
Thicket-forming shrub. White flowers are succeeded by waxy white berries. Bark is reddish.

Salal
Gaultheria shallon
To 4 ft. (1.2 m)
Shrub has delicate urn-shaped flowers that are succeeded by edible berries. Leaves are leathery.

Serviceberry
Amelanchier spp.
To 15 ft. (4.5 m)
White, 5-petalled flowers bloom April–July and are succeeded by purplish, sweet berries.

Pacific Ninebark
Physocarpus capitatus
To 14 ft. (4.2 m)
Flowers bloom in rounded clusters. Papery bark is shredding.

Kinnikinnick
Arctostaphylos uva-ursi
To 12 in. (30 cm)
Pinkish, bell-shaped flowers are succeeded by red-orange, mealy berries. Also known as bearberry.

Snowberry
Symphoricarpos albus
To 4 ft. (1.2 m)
Waxy white berries persist into autumn.

Red-Flowering Currant
Ribes sanguineum
To 13 ft. (4 m)
Leaves are up to 3 in. (8 cm) long with 5 lobes. Dangling red flower clusters are succeeded by dark purple, oval berries.

Black Huckleberry
Vaccinium ovatum
To 10 ft. (3 m)
Bell-shaped pinkish flowers are succeeded by edible black berries.

Devil's Club
Oplopanax horridus
To 10 ft. (3 m)
Spiny plant has large, maple-like leaves with 7–9 toothed lobes. Berries persist into winter.

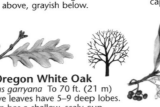

Poison Hemlock
Conium maculatum
To 10 ft. (3 m)
Leaves are parsley-like.
Flowers bloom in flat-topped clusters.
All parts of the plant are deadly poisonous.

Queen Anne's Lace
Daucus carota
To 4 ft. (1.2 m)
Flower clusters become cup-shaped as they age.

White Trillium
Trillium ovatum
To 16 in. (40 cm)
Large 3-petalled flower is framed by a whorl of 3 broad leaves.

Cotton Grass
Eriophorum spp.
To 4 ft. (1.2 m)
Distinctive fluffy seed heads have long, silky hairs.

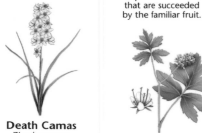

Stinging Nettle
Urtica spp. To 10 ft. (3 m)
Plant prickles eject a stinging toxin on contact.

Death Camas
Zigadenus spp.
To 3 ft. (90 cm)
Star-shaped, green-centered flowers bloom in a long terminal cluster. Plant is highly poisonous.

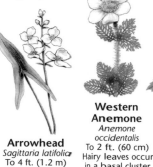

Arrowhead
Sagittaria latifolia
To 4 ft. (1.2 m)
Aquatic plant has arrow-shaped leaves.

Western Anemone
Anemone occidentalis
To 2 ft. (60 cm)
Hairy leaves occur in a basal cluster and a single stem cluster.

Three-leaved Foamflower
Tiarella trifoliata
To 16 in. (40 cm)
Tiny white flowers look like flecks of foam at a distance.

Indian Pipe
Monotropa uniflora
To 10 in. (25 cm)
Waxy white plant is parasitic on other plants in shady woods.

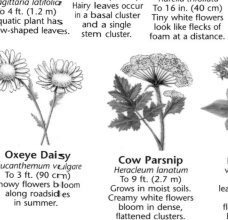

Oxeye Daisy
Leucanthemum vulgare
To 3 ft. (90 cm)
Showy flowers bloom along roadsides in summer.

Cow Parsnip
Heracleum lanatum
To 9 ft. (2.7 m)
Grows in moist soils.
Creamy white flowers bloom in dense, flattened clusters.

English Ivy
Hedera helix
Evergreen, climbing vine. Alternate leaves are dark green and leathery, with 3–5 lobes. Small yellow-green flowers are succeeded by fleshy dark fruits.

Wild Strawberry
Fragaria spp.
Stems to 8 in. (20 cm)
Creeping plant has 5-petalled flowers that are succeeded by the familiar fruit.

Field Bindweed
Convolvulus arvensis
To 3 ft. (90 cm)
Told by arrowhead-shaped leaves and white to pink, funnel-shaped flowers. A noxious weed.

Miner's Lettuce
Claytonia perfoliata
To 14 in. (35 cm)
Flowers are white or pink.

Pacific Waterleaf
Hydrophyllum tenuipes
To 2 ft. (60 cm)
Greenish-white to lavender, flowers have 5 conspicuous stamen extending far beyond the petal margin.

Bunchberry
Cornus canadensis
To 8 in. (20 cm)
Leaves grow in whorls of 4–6.

Pearly Everlasting
Anaphalis margaritacea
To 3 ft. (90 cm)
Creamy flowers bloom in large terminal clusters.

Vanilla Leaf
Achlys triphylla
To 20 in. (50 cm)

Yarrow
Achillea millefolium
To 3 ft. (90 cm)
Leaves are fern-like.

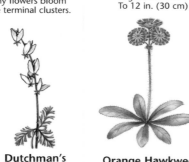

Bear Grass
Xerophyllum tenax
To 5 ft. (1.5 m)
Star-like creamy flowers bloom in a dense terminal spike.

Dutchman's Breeches
Dicentra cucullaria
To 12 in. (30 cm)
Spurred flowers resemble trousers.

Shepherd's Purse
Capsella bursa-pastoris
To 16 in. (40 cm)
Widespread invasive weed is named for its flattened, heart-shaped seed pods. Note basal rosette of lobed leaves.

White Clover
Trifolium repens
Stems to 10 in. (25 cm)
Creeping plant has 3-part leaves and rounded, white flowers. The common lawn clover. Invasive.

Marsh Marigold
Caltha leptosepala
To 12 in. (30 cm)
Found in mountain marshes and wet meadows.

Yellow Skunk Cabbage
Lysichiton americanus
To 20 in. (50 cm)
Common in swampy areas.

Pond Lily
Nuphar spp.
To 4 in. (10 cm)
Floating aquatic plant.

Tiger Lily
Lilium columbianum
To 4 ft. (1.2 m)

Glacier Lily
Erythronium grandiflorum
To 12 in. (30 cm)

Yellow Monkeyflower
Mimulus guttatus
To 3 ft. (90 cm)
Flowers are trumpet-shaped.

Violet
Viola spp. To 16 in. (40 cm)
Leaves are typically heart-shaped and slightly toothed. Flower color varies from yellow to purple and white.

Orange Hawkweed
Hieracium aurantiacum
To 2 ft. (60 cm)
Hairy plant has leaves clustered at its base. A noxious weed.

Common Dandelion
Taraxacum officinale
To 20 in. (50 cm)

Common St. John's Wort
Hypericum perforatum
To 30 in. (75 cm)
Widespread weed is found in waste areas.

Yellow Flag
Iris pseudacorus
To 3 ft. (90 cm)

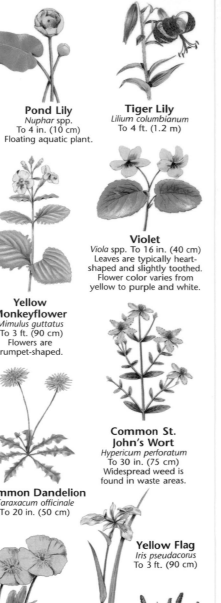

Blanketflower
Gaillardia aristata
To 3 ft. (90 cm)

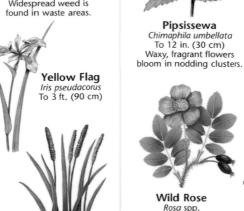

Buttercup
Ranunculus spp.
To 3 ft. (90 cm)
Flower petals are waxy to the touch.

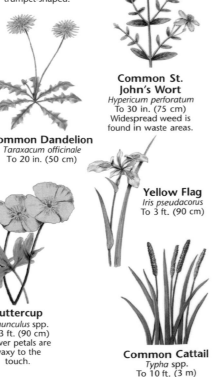

Common Cattail
Typha spp.
To 10 ft. (3 m)

Common Mullein
Verbascum thapsus
To 7 ft. (2.1 m)
Common roadside weed.

Pitcher Plant
Darlingtonia californica
To 3 ft. (90 cm)

Butter-and-Eggs
Linaria vulgaris
To 3 ft. (90 cm)
Spurred flowers have a patch of orange in the throat. Invasive.

Blazing Star
Mentzelia laevicaulis
To 5 ft. (1.5 m)

Wild Ginger
Asarum canadense
To 12 in. (30 cm)
Flowers arise at base of two leaves.

Redwood Sorrel
Oxalis oregana
To 7 in. (18 cm)
Note clover-like leaves.

Pacific Star Flower
Trientalis latifolia
To 10 in. (25 cm)

Pipsissewa
Chimaphila umbellata
To 12 in. (30 cm)
Waxy, fragrant flowers bloom in nodding clusters.

Red Monkeyflower
Mimulus lewisii
To 3 ft. (90 cm)

Pink Rhododendron
Rhododendron macrophyllum
To 25 ft. (7.5 m)
Flowering shrub.

Wild Rose
Rosa spp.
To 13 ft. (3.9 m)
Flowers are succeeded by fruits called "hips."

Fringecups
Tellima grandiflora
To 30 in. (75 cm)

Fairy Slipper
Calypso bulbosa
To 8 in. (20 cm)
Found in damp woods.

Twinflower
Linnaea borealis
To 4 in. (10 cm)

Striped Coral Root
Corallorhiza striata
To 20 in. (50 cm)
Flowers have dark stripes.

Water Smartweed
Polygonum amphibium
Stems to 4 ft. (1.2 m) long.
Aquatic plant blooms in nearshore waters.

Sea Blush
Plectritis congesta
To 3 ft. (90 cm)
Blooms in dense carpets from Feb.–May.

Firewheel
Gaillardia pulchella
To 2 ft. (60 cm)

Beardtongue
Penstemon spp.
To 2 ft. (60 cm)
Lower lip and throat of flower is "bearded" with fine hairs.

Western Columbine
Aquilegia formosa
To 3 ft. (90 cm)
Note long spurs.

Roseroot
Sedum roseum
To 12 in. (30 cm)
Mat-forming plant.

Western Bleeding Heart
Dicentra formosa
To 18 in. (45 cm)

Round-leaved Sundew
Drosera rotundifolia
To 10 in. (25 cm)
Bog plant has leaves covered with sticky droplets.

Bull Thistle
Cirsium vulgare
To 5 ft. (1.8 m)

Shooting Star
Dodecatheon spp.
To 2 ft. (60 cm)

Elephant Heads
Pedicularis groenlandica
To 31 in. (78 cm)
Flowers are shaped like elephant heads.

Fireweed
Chamerion angustifolium
To 5 ft. (1.5 m)
Common in open woodlands and waste areas.

Foxglove
Digitalis purpurea
To 5 ft. (1.5 m)
Invasive.

Harebell
Campanula rotundifolia
To 40 in. (1 m)

Wild Bergamot
Monarda fistulosa
To 4 ft. (1.2 m)

Bluebells
Mertensia paniculata
To 30 in. (75 cm)

Aster
Aster spp.
To 5 ft. (1.5 m)

Piggyback Plant
Tolmiea menziesii
To 12 in. (30 cm)
Has distinctive, awl-shaped purplish-brown petals.

Larkspur
Delphinium spp.
To 6 ft. (1.8 m)
5-part flowers have prominent spurs.

Monkshood
Aconitum columbianum
To 6 ft. (1.8 m)
Deep blue flowers resemble a monk's habit.

Vetch
Vicia spp.
To 6 ft. (1.8 m)
Climbing or sprawling plant has purple to pink pea-shaped flowers.

Blue Flag
Iris spp.
To 3 ft. (90 cm)

Lupine
Lupinus spp.
To 3 ft. (90 cm)
Note star-shaped leaves.

Blue-eyed Grass
Sisyrinchium angustifolium
To 20 in. (50 cm)

Sticky Geranium
Geranium viscosissimum
To 3 ft. (90 cm)
Leaf stems and flower stalks are sticky to the touch.

    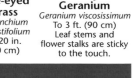 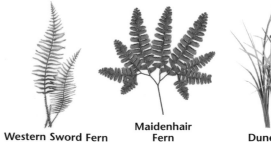

Western Sword Fern
Polystichum munitum
To 5 ft. (1.5 m)

Maidenhair Fern
Adiantum pedatum
To 2 ft. (60 cm)

Dune Sedge
Carex obnupta
To 5 ft. (1.5 m)